STEAM ON THE SOUTHERN AND WESTERN

A GLIMPSE OF THE 1950s and 1960s

STEAM ON THE SOUTHERN AND WESTERN

A GLIMPSE OF THE 1950s and 1960s

DAVID KNAPMAN

PEN & SWORD
TRANSPORT

First published in Great Britain in 2018 by
Pen and Sword Transport

An imprint of Pen & Sword Books Limited
47 Church Street , Barnsley, South Yorkshire
S70 2AS

ISBN: 978 1 47389 240 8

A CIP catalogue record for this book is available from the British Library

Typeset by Aura Technology and Software Services, India
Printed and bound in India by Replika Pvt. Ltd.

Pen & Sword Books Limited incorporates the imprints of Atlas, Archaeology, Aviation, Discovery,
Family History, Fiction, History, Maritime, Military, Military Classics, Politics, Select, Transport, True Crime,
Air World, Frontline Publishing, Leo Cooper, Remember When, Seaforth Publishing,
The Praetorian Press, Wharncliffe Local History, Wharncliffe Transport,
Wharncliffe True Crime and White Owl.

For a complete list of Pen & Sword titles please contact
PEN & SWORD BOOKS LIMITED
47 Church Street, Barnsley, South Yorkshire, S70 2AS, United Kingdom
E-mail: enquiries@pen-and-sword.co.uk
Website: www.pen-and-sword.co.uk

CONTENTS

Introduction 7

PART ONE: SOUTHERN REGION

Chapter 1   Betchworth Station 11

Chapter 2   Brockham Crossing 17

Chapter 3   Guildford 21

Chapter 4   Ashford (Kent) 27

Chapter 5   Kent Coast, a brief visit...33

Chapter 6   Waterloo Station and Environs 35

Chapter 7   The Hayling Island Branch 43

Chapter 8   The Hawkhurst Branch..47

Chapter 9   The Kent and East Sussex Railway 50

Chapter 10   The Bluebell Railway 53

Chapter 11   The Isle of Wight...57

Chapter 12   The Lymington Branch 65

Chapter 13   Brockenhurst to Broadstone..69

Chapter 14   The Somerset and Dorset Joint Railway.........................72

PART TWO: WESTERN REGION

Chapter 15   Paddington...80

Chapter 16   Old Oak Common Shed 89

Chapter 17   Reading Station and Shed 92

Chapter 18   Oxford 99

Chapter 19   Tiverton and Hemyock 109

Chapter 20   Festiniog Railway Special 25 April 1964 112

Chapter 21   Hereford 116

Chapter 22   Welsh Week, June 1964 122

Chapter 23   Barry Island 139

Chapter 24   A Glimpse of the Future! 142

INTRODUCTION

There is no doubt that the steam locomotive continues to fascinate both young and old people today and the lineside audiences for the 2016 rebirth of *Flying Scotsman* lend huge support to that view.

So, why another book of railway photographs? Given that my interest started at a young age, covering the period of the late 1950s to the end of steam, it seemed opportune to take up John Scott-Morgan's challenge to produce a book using the black and white negatives in my collection.

Living close to the Reading to Redhill line near Betchworth meant that it was an obvious magnet of interest within easy cycling distance. As a schoolboy in those days, the film budget was hard earned and so travel away from the local line was a rare event. A few Brownie box camera pictures pass muster for inclusion in this book, but a 1959 purchase of an Agfa 35mm camera, with a faster shutter speed, laid the foundation for more photography. This book will not be all about the glamourous main line expresses, but a broader collection of railway experiences, which in their own way will hopefully give pleasure and stir memories for the reader.

The early delights on the Reading to Redhill line produced three 'D' class 4-4-0s including 31737 in 1958, whilst early expeditions with my enthusiast father, J.J. Knapman, included a splendid run on the Bristolian with 'Castle' 4-6-0 5043 *Earl of Mount Edgcumbe* and the Kentish Belle to Margate, when the return run to Victoria was headed by 'West Country' 4-6-2 34092 *City of Wells*. Contact with locomotives subsequently preserved seemed to be the order of the day.

I include here a paternal photograph of me, in school cap, with my brother, in the cab of 5043 at Bristol Temple Meads after the run on the *Bristolian* on 14 August 1958. Grateful thanks to the driver, standing at the back of the cab, for allowing us aboard.

(*J.J. Knapman*)

Fifty one years later, I had the privilege of being allowed into the cab of the same locomotive by Bob Meanley after I had shown him the 1958 photograph. There were some teasing comments about 'That Cap' in the 1958 picture, as you can imagine!

This book will be in two parts, Southern and Western, with chapters setting out the photographs, which are intended to provide a flavour for each selected location, and each photograph will be supported by an explanatory caption. In due course, a companion volume will be produced for Eastern and Midland Steam.

It gives me enormous pleasure to share my photographs with you, and I hope readers will derive similar enjoyment as they digest the contents of this book.

David Knapman May 2018.

(Bob Meanley)

PART ONE

SOUTHERN REGION

CHAPTER 1

BETCHWORTH STATION

Betchworth Station is located beneath the North Downs in Surrey, between Deepdene and Reigate on the ex-Southern Railway's Reading to Redhill line. The station building originally dates from 1849 and in the 1930s the signal and level crossing controls were housed in the station building in the room overlooking the westbound platform. The signalmen were generally helpful to youthful enthusiasts, and Paddy, in particular, would advise when non-timetabled special workings were due. More time was spent at this location than at home during the holidays! Betchworth Station had the distinction of a link to the Dorking Greystone Lime Company by means of a standard gauge siding so that lime products could be transported by the national network.

The first picture taken with the 35mm camera depicts Maunsell 'U' 2-6-0 31616 with a set of coaches by the same designer. The train is a mid-morning departure for Reading. Note the dip in the platform levels by the first coach. The photographer is standing on the platform extension, which probably saw little use. To the left of the picture is the siding to the Dorking Greystone Lime Company network. 28 June 1959.

This picture is of interest on a number of counts. The train is the afternoon working to Margate from the Midlands. It was running late and the signalman was concerned about its progress. Instead of the customary British Railways (BR) standard '4MT' 2-6-0, the motive power was being manfully provided by 'L1' 4-4-0 31786, a substantial task for such a locomotive over this hilly route. At the end of the platform are the diagram and levers for the ground frame used to access the Lime Company siding, the connection to which is seen at the right. 28 June 1959.

On a hot summer afternoon, ex-London Brighton and South Coast railway (LBSCR) 'C2X' 0-6-0 32450 arrives at Betchworth with a brake van in tow. This working is to collect a single wagon of lime from the Lime Company siding. The locomotive is passing the signal room in the station building. 4 July 1959.

The shunter can just be seen gently releasing the lime wagon brake to allow the wagon to reach the main line connection, by gravity. 4 July 1959.

Having shunted the wagon and guard's van into the appropriate order, 'C2X' 0-6-0 32450 takes its enlarged train away to Redhill. Not exactly an economic proposition, but full of interest. 4 July 1959.

My first ever railway photograph depicts the Dorking Greystone Lime company's 0-4-0T No. 3, *Captain Baxter*. The locomotive was built by Fletcher Jennings & Co of Whitehaven in Cumbria and became part of the Lime Company's fleet in 1871. The locomotive is seen at the top of the freight exchange siding, whilst the main line is in the cutting to the right of the chalk covered employee. August 1958.

An example of unusual workings on the Reading to Redhill line is depicted passing Betchworth Station. 'River' rebuild 'U' 2-6-0 31807 is taking an out of steam 'Q1' 0-6-0 in the direction of Redhill, for mechanical attention. Note the Lime Company's buildings above the locomotives. These buildings housed *Coffeepot* and *Captain Baxter*. November 1958.

Ex-London and South Western Railway (LSWR) 'T9' 4-4-0 30732 has arrived at Betchworth Station with an afternoon train for Redhill. The driver is sharing a joke with the signalman. The delight of the Reading to Redhill line was the variety of motive power which appeared unexpectedly. 4 April 1959.

On a lovely summer's day in August 1959, Maunsell 'U' 2-6-0 31625 pulls into Betchworth Station with a morning train for Redhill, formed of BR mark one stock. The locomotive is now preserved and I had the privilege of driving this engine on the Mid Hants Railway for a day. Right hand drive 31625 has a modified BR chimney and new frames construction.

It is 1 April 1963 and 'Manor' 4-6-0 7813 *Freshford Manor* is entering Betchworth Station with the two coach 11.20am train from Redhill to Reading. This train had been delayed by a preceding freight, but the timetable provided a lay-over at Guildford, so recovery time was available. Ex-Great Western Railway (GWR) locomotives had long worked over the Reading to Redhill line to provide route knowledge when working summer excursion and holiday trains from the Midlands to the South Coast.

CHAPTER 2

BROCKHAM CROSSING

Brockham Crossing is about two miles west of Betchworth Station and a crossing keeper's house was located there, together with a train on line indicator, which usefully advised when a train was en route. The crossing provided an access to the chalk pits and lime works, although latterly just to Bishops Cottages via Chalk Pit Lane.

This was a good location to see eastbound trains climbing towards Betchworth, whilst westbound trains would rush past comparatively quietly. The crossing keeper's house has long been demolished and the location is now rather overgrown. However, we can look at some pictures of tidier times and see how steam was handling local trains.

On a misty 4 April 1960, 'Schools' 4-4-0 30907 *Dulwich* drifts past Brockham Crossing with a morning train for Guildford. The train indicator on the crossing house can just be seen to the left of the trespassers board.

A day later, the sun is out and Maunsell 'U' 2-6-0 31628 is heading briskly for Redhill at Brockham Crossing with a morning train comprised of Bulleid coaches. The over bridge seen down the line marks half the viewing distance from this location.

To emphasise the line's motive power variety, Guildford shedded 'M7' 0-4-4T 30132 is taking a set of Maunsell coaches towards Redhill on a morning train at Brockham Crossing. 12 April 1960.

'Manor' 4-6-0 7824 *Iford Manor* is taking the 4.04pm train from Redhill to Reading under the bridge mentioned in the photograph of 31628. This is a return working by 7824 to get it to home territory after working a train from the Midlands earlier. Brockham Crossing is situated at the line's curve in the distance and the cottages marking Chalk Pit Lane are seen at the left of the picture. Note the splendid telegraph pole route. This scene today is much covered by vegetation. 22 August 1959.

Brockham Crossing is host to 'N' 2-6-0 31864 as it heads a substantial freight train towards Redhill on 19 July 1959. The locomotive has a replacement BR chimney and carries two route discs as if it was operating a local passenger train.

And finally … 'N' 2-6-0 No 31831 is working very hard past Brockham Crossing, heading for Redhill, with the Locomotive Club of Great Britain (LCGB) Maunsell Commemorative Railtour, marking the expected end of steam power on the Reading to Redhill line. 3 January 1965.

CHAPTER 3

GUILDFORD

Guildford Station boasted a steam shed code 70C, where locomotives for the Reading to Redhill services were based. The station provided the change point for trains to Redhill, Reading, Horsham, Portsmouth, Effingham Junction and Woking as well as destinations further afield. Guildford station provided the opportunity to see a variety of locomotives and not just of Southern Railway origin.

On 1 April 1963, the station is a stopping point for 'Manor' 4-6-0 7813 *Freshford Manor* which has arrived from Redhill with a two coach train for Reading.

The overbridge at Guildford Station provides a different view of 7813 as it and its crew rest during the lay over before departure time for Reading. The property, Freshford Manor, is located near Bath and was listed in the Domesday Book. 7813 met its doomsday on 10 May 1965, when it was withdrawn from service. 1 April 1963.

Staple fare for Guildford is locally shedded 'U' 2-6-0 31633 which has revised draughting arrangements, a BR chimney and renewed frames. This locomotive was withdrawn just two months later. 12 October 1963.

Hidden by the 'Manor's train at Guildford is 'S15' 4-6-0 30840 making a move from Guildford shed after servicing. 30840 does not appear to have a shedplate, but was allocated to Feltham at the time. These locomotives were used on Feltham to Reading freights. 1 April 1963.

'USA' tanks had been a feature of Guildford shed for a number of years and here is 30072 basking in the Autumn sunshine. 30072 is preserved at the Keighley and Worth Valley Railway. 12 October 1963.

A newcomer to Guildford is '82XXX' 2-6-2T 82027, which had been transferred from the North East, when 82026,7,8 and 9 arrived at 70C during September 1963. Note the large style number on the bunker side. 12 October 1963.

A long-term resident of Guildford shed is 'U' 2-6-0 31797, which is trying to find the sunshine as it heads a Redhill train. This is one of the 'River' 2-6-4T rebuilds and still sports a Maunsell chimney. I travelled on this train as far as Gomshall and noted that the engine worked well on the hilly section to that station. 12 October 1963.

On 12 October 1963, the afternoon Horsham branch train is leaving a sunlit Guildford station headed by Ivatt-designed 2-6-2T 41326. Note the Gill Sans style digits on the front number plate on this Brighton shedded locomotive. The delightfully rural Guildford to Horsham branch opened throughout on 2 October 1865 and closed just short of its centenary on 14 June 1965.

CHAPTER 4

ASHFORD (KENT)

In 1960, visits to Ashford Station provided a considerable surprise to me aged fifteen, in the amount of railway activity and the variety of motive power to be seen. Routes to London, Dover, Maidstone, Canterbury and Hastings brought an interesting selection of trains to and from those directions. Ashford Locomotive works was built near to the station in 1847 and extended later in the twentieth century. Locomotive building work ceased here in 1962, but other railway vehicles continued to be repaired at the works. This chapter provides a selection of motive power seen at the station and some scenes from within the works.

Maunsell 'N' 2-6-0 31859 is passing Ashford Station with a short freight train bound for South London. The 2-6-0 retains its Maunsell chimney. The engineman is having an easy time as he surveys an almost deserted station. 25 July 1960.

On the same date, an 'H' 0-4-4T 31542 arrives in the up side bay platform at Ashford with a train from the Hastings line. The smartly dressed driver is sporting a tie, an unusual item of attire on the footplate! 25 July 1960.

Nicely turned out rebuilt 'West Country' 4-6-2 34014 *Budleigh Salterton* arrives at Ashford with a Dover-bound express, comprising Maunsell, Bulleid and BR coaching stock. 27 July 1960.

Unrebuilt 'Battle of Britain' 4-6-2 34089 *602 Squadron* makes an impressive sight as it passes under Ashford's signal gantry with a London bound special boat train, with two luggage vans at the head of the train. 25 July 1960.

Brighton shed's ex LBSCR 'K' 2-6-0 32342 arrives light engine at the bay platform. These competent moguls were liked by enginemen and worked both passenger and freight turns. They had dual braking systems and note the Westinghouse pump. Reputedly, they were designer Lawson Billinton's favourite design. These Brighton engines were not often used outside the Central Section of the Southern Region. 27 July 1960.

A delightful study of multiple jet blast piped 'Schools' 4-4-0 30929 *Malvern* bringing a stopping train from the Dover direction into Ashford Station. The locomotive is allocated to Bricklayers Arms shed and the train comprises a set of Bulleid coaches with a van at each end of the set. 27 July 1960.

The erecting shop in Ashford works is busy with the repair of 'Q1' 0-6-0 33036, 'Schools' 4-4-0 30936 *Cranleigh* and an 'N' 2-6-0. The visit was occasioned by an Ian Allan tour to Ashford and Eastleigh works on 5 April 1961.

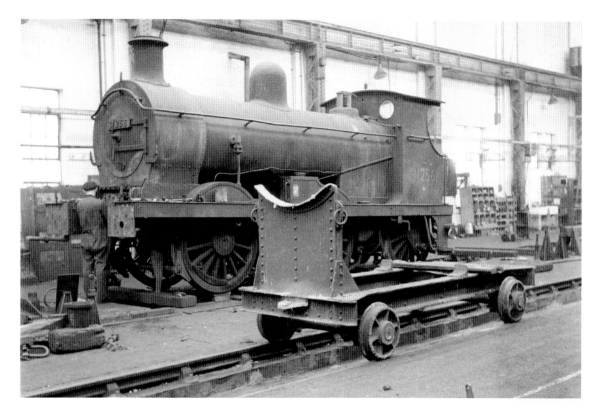

A Wainwright-designed 'C' 0-6-0 31256 is also receiving attention, requiring it to be in an elevated position. The supports under the locomotive's front wheels look rather precarious and the smoke box door looks to be in need of refurbishment. 5 April 1961.

The Ian Allan special brought ex LSWR 'T9' 4-4-0 30117 and Southern Railway (SR) 'E1' 4-4-0 31019 to Ashford from London, Cannon Street. These venerable 4-4-0's were replaced by 'Schools' 4-4-0 30909 *St Paul's* for the onward journey to Woking via Guildford. 5 April 1961.

A going away view of the 'T9' and 'E1' passing northwards through Ashford on the through road. 5 April 1961. The special train provided a feast of 4-4-0s on the day, for the final journey from Woking to Eastleigh and return to London was hauled by 'Schools' 30913 *Christ's Hospital*.

CHAPTER 5

KENT COAST, A BRIEF VISIT

On 25 February 1962, the LCGB ran a special train to Ramsgate via the Kent Coast line and return via Ashford, to mark the end of steam power out of Victoria Station. The motive power in 1962 was 'King Arthur' 4-6-0 30782 *Sir Brian*, which handed over to 'Schools' 4-4-0 30926 *Repton* at Ashford. As is the way of things, my camera failed on this special occasion, but these two photographs survived.

My place in the rear coach provided a position to obtain this photograph of *Sir Brian* at the top of Grosvenor Bank on departure from Victoria. No banker of course. The carriage sheds look particularly empty.

'King Arthur' 4-6-0 30782 *Sir Brian* is being serviced at Ramsgate station amidst a crowd of admirers. The fireman is moving coal forward in the tender and thankfully there are no high vis vests!

CHAPTER 6

WATERLOO STATION AND ENVIRONS

This chapter will encompass Waterloo, Vauxhall, Clapham Junction and Wimbledon. The age of locomotives working in this area spanned half a century of design and were found working empty stock trains, expresses and special workings. If only time and income had been sufficient to record more, but for me, still at school, these pictures capture some of the great trains that could be seen at the time. Waterloo is said to be the premier terminus for the Southern Region with steam turns to the West of England, Southampton and Bournemouth as well as numerous destinations for the intensive third rail electric services.

On 2 December 1962, two '0298' Beattie 2-4-0 well tanks 30585 and 30587 were found at Waterloo, well away from their normal West Country location. In their very early days, such engines worked London suburban trains, so to welcome them back to London was a delight. The Railway Correspondence and Travel Society (RCTS) and the Stephenson Locomotive Society (SLS) sponsored this special train and the two locomotives are backing down to their train at Waterloo on this glorious frosty day.

Here the two Beatties leave Waterloo having gained headboard and discs. The train is bound for Hampton Court and Wimbledon. It was reported that all three Beattie well tanks came to London for this train, although 30586 was not used.

30585 and 30587 have Waterloo Station signal box as a backdrop as they head west in very confident fashion.

It was possible to catch an electric service train to Wimbledon to overtake the special train, and the two Beattie well tanks are entering that station as they tour the London suburbs. 'H16' 4-6-2 tank 30517 was also involved in this tour, taking the train from Wimbledon to Chessington South and return. 2 December 1962.

At Waterloo, a tender-first view of grubby 'Merchant Navy' 35022 *Holland-America Line*. It is waiting signal clearance to back down to Nine Elms shed. Coal has spilled over the tender edge, which forms a hazard for tender-first running. 5 January 1961.

Also at Waterloo, a veteran 'M7' 0-4-4T 30245 is marshalling parcels vans. These locomotives covered a huge amount of empty stock workings between Clapham Junction and Waterloo. Departing expresses could expect a shove from an 'M7' to help them get away over the brief hump at the end of the platforms. This engine is now preserved in the National Collection. 5 January 1961.

'Merchant Navy' 35029 *Ellerman Lines* is getting into its stride with the Atlantic Coast Express at Vauxhall, 1.3 miles from Waterloo. The train, of Bulleid stock, will be divided in the West Country to serve destinations including Exeter, Ilfracombe, Torrington, Bude, Padstow and Plymouth. This locomotive is preserved in sectioned condition in the National Railway Museum. 8 September 1961.

'Battle of Britain' class unrebuilt light pacific 34054 *Lord Beaverbrook* is taking a West of England express through Vauxhall on 8 September 1961. The locomotive appears to be in presentable condition with no steam leaks.

It is always a pleasure to see a 'Lord Nelson' in action, but it is a pity that 30852 *Sir Walter Raleigh* could not have been better turned out to head a Waterloo to Southampton Docks boat train through Vauxhall. This locomotive completed 1.25 million miles before withdrawal in February 1962. 8 September 1961.

It was the day for grubby locomotives. 35012 *United States Lines*, a 'Merchant Navy' 4-6-2, heads a splendid rake of Pullman cars forming the Bournemouth Belle. Note the art deco style lamp shades on the platform lights. The final Bournemouth Belle train ran on 9 July 1967. 8 September 1961.

Urie-designed 'H16' 4-6-2T 30520 is the last of the class of five locomotives originally built for cross-London freight work from Feltham yard. Latterly, they were employed on empty carriage workings and here 30520 is passing Vauxhall station with empty stock heading for Clapham sidings. 8 September 1961.

Illuminated by the sun, light engine Urie designed 'S15' 4-6-0 30507 is backing down to Waterloo Station past Vauxhall prior to an afternoon working. This locomotive was built in late 1920 and is paired with a Urie double bogie 5000 gallon tender. 30507 was withdrawn in December 1963 having run 1.25 million miles. Sister engine 30506 is preserved on the Mid Hants Railway. 8 September 1961.

On 2 December 1962, 'Merchant Navy' pacific 35028 *Clan Line* is powering through Clapham Junction with a Pullman train, most likely the Bournemouth Belle. Use of the headboard by this time had become intermittent. 35028 is a stalwart of the preservation era, mainly involved with Pullman haulage even now and demonstrating an impressive reliability.

How is this for variety? Two Dugald Drummond-designed locomotives head the Blue Belle special train from Victoria to the Bluebell Railway through Clapham Junction. Caledonian Railway 4-2-2 123 built in 1886 and LSWR 'T9' 4-4-0 120 built in 1899 form a superb double header. The departing electric unit clears the scene just in time! 15 September 1963.

CHAPTER 7

THE HAYLING ISLAND BRANCH

In the early 1960s, some of the well-known branch lines in the country were coming under threat of closure following the Beeching report on reshaping Britain's railways. Just such a line was the popular Havant to Hayling Island line to the east of Portsmouth. This line supported the use of ex LBSCR 'A1X Terrier' 0-6-0 tank locomotives, which were suitably light motive power for the 1,100 feet long timber Langston harbour swing bridge. The line was opened to traffic in July 1867 and leased to the LBSCR in 1872, which arrangement was disputed by the neighbouring LSWR and it was not until 1922 that the LBSCR completely absorbed the line's operations. The 'Terrier' tanks remained in charge of the line until closure on 4 November 1963. The branch suffered from road competition, with investment being made in the local road system, but not in the railway. The pictures are from my visit on 22 August 1962.

32661 is coupled to the Hayling Island train at Havant Station. The four-track layout of the main station can be seen to the right. Havant Station was modified to this layout during electrification just before the Second World War.

'A1X' Terrier 0-6-0T 32661 is at Havant Station in the bay platform for Hayling Island trains, taking refreshment as a crew member attends to its coal supply. 32661 started its working life in 1875 for the LBSCR London suburban services as 61 *Sutton*. It was the last 'Terrier' to leave London to work at country locations and the last of the class to be scrapped by BR in September 1963.

The junction for Hayling Island is shown here with the island line curving right past a substantial water tower with the signal box, governing main and branch lines, to the left.

This is a view of Langston Harbour Bridge and the harbour taken from the Hayling Island train. The bridge signal box can just be made out halfway along the structure. The signal is the Langston Bridge down home signal and the post also carries the up distant signal for Langston Station.

This is the terminus at Hayling Island with a young intending passenger. The end of the coach in the main platform belongs to a non-gangway suburban coach.

32661 is carrying a spark arrester and its coal bunker has extra capacity as shown by the higher bunker coal rails. The locomotive has run round its train at Hayling Island prior to coupling up for the return to Havant. The rail post for the starter signal is left and 32661 is passing a substantial permanent way hut on the right.

CHAPTER 8

THE HAWKHURST BRANCH

The Paddock Wood to Hawkhurst branch had as its resident engineer Colonel Holman Stephens, who had completed the line in September 1893. In trying to view other branch lines under threat from road traffic in the 1960s, I was just too late to see passenger traffic here as the line had closed in June 1961. School holidays did not always coincide with the right months in which to see the action! These pictures of Hawkhurst Station were taken on a dull 23 July 1961, with the majority of the infrastructure still intact, before demolition.

The terminus at Hawkhurst and the station building, with track still intact, looking towards the bufferstops. The station building and bufferstops had only been repainted three months before; a sure closure warning!

A view of the station showing the South Eastern and Chatham Railway (SECR) shunt signal, signal box, water tank, departure signals and locomotive shed. The 46¼ milepost from London is tucked into the station fencing.

The departure lines and signals, locomotive shed and approach signals in the distance. Hop poles are stacked in the yard to the right of the picture.

As the station was deserted, it was a golden opportunity to climb the approach bracket signal to photograph the view of the station. The layout looks ready to receive a push-pull train headed by an 'H' 0-4-4 tank, but sadly it was not to be.

CHAPTER 9

THE KENT AND EAST SUSSEX RAILWAY

The Kent and East Sussex Railway history from opening in 1900 by Colonel Holman Stephens to final closure by British Railways in June 1961 and the reincarnation as a preserved railway is well known. Visits to the line on 24 and 25 July 1961 found the track in place, albeit rusty, with the railway waiting forlornly for its next step in life. I was fortunate to have a ride in the brake van of a freight train from Northiam to Mill Lane, Robertsbridge, hauled by Drewry diesel D2276. This ride is recorded in John Scott-Morgan's book *An Illustrated History of the Kent and East Sussex Railway*, so on these later visits it was pleasing to find so much of the infrastructure still complete.

Here is a view of Tenterden station yard with the station building in the distance, looking towards Robertsbridge. The Ministry of Supply owned the Nissen huts on the right and the former island platform has long gone.

What a survivor! A Kent and East Sussex Railway trespassers notice at Tenterden. The board carries the name of W.H. Austen, who was general manager of the railway from 1932 to 1948 when the line was absorbed by British Railways.

This is the site of Wittersham Road station looking towards Tenterden. The station here had been demolished soon after closure of passenger services in 1954. The preserved railway has rebuilt Wittersham Road station, with a passing loop, but the chances of this happening in 1961 seemed very remote indeed!

Northiam Station basking quietly in the sunshine; this view is looking towards Robertsbridge. The 'WHISTLE' board has its back to the camera and the level crossings were unprotected and the trains were restricted to 10mph, when the line was in use.

CHAPTER 10

THE BLUEBELL RAILWAY

The Bluebell Railway emerged from the closure of the Lewes to East Grinstead Railway and the history of the original railway and its preservation successor has been extensively recorded. The line opened in August 1882 and after various attempts by British Railways to close the line, the last day of operation occurred on 16 March 1958. Almost exactly a year later, a meeting took place to set up the first stages for preservation of this railway, the first service commencing on 7 August 1960. It is timely to include some photographs here of the emerging Bluebell Railway in the early days of preservation, to show that whilst other branch lines were being closed, it was possible, by the amazing efforts of volunteers, to bring transport, pleasure and a boost to the local economy. Hopefully these photographs taken on the 4 August 1964 are of historical interest fifty plus years later.

In mellow afternoon sunshine, the ex-LSWR Adams designed 4-4-2 radial tank 488 (BR 30583) brings a two-coach train into Horsted Keynes station, at the junction with the Ardingly branch. Note the conductor rails on the Ardingly branch which was closed in October 1963. The coaching stock comprises an ex SECR ten compartment non-corridor coach and the ex-London & North Western Railway observation saloon.

The Adams tank at rest at Horsted Keynes station, before running round its train to return to Sheffield Park. It is a great pity that this elegant locomotive has not been steamed for a very long time.

The ex-North London Railway 0-6-0 tank 2650 is in steam and engaged in shunting work at Horsted Keynes. This locomotive is also out of use at the time of writing. Ironically, it was used in part of the track removal by British Railways, north of Horsted Keynes.

At Sheffield Park station, ex-GWR 'Dukedog' 4-4-0 9017 ponders its future. Having worked well on the Bluebell Railway and appropriately visited the Llangollen Railway, this locomotive is out of ticket in 2017 and rests in Sheffield Park museum.

Also outside the locomotive shed at Sheffield Park is ex LBSCR 'E4' 0-6-2T 473 *Birch Grove*, awaiting a turn of duty. 473 is splendidly turned out in Brighton Umber livery and was to be in use a few days after my visit.

Viewed from the train, the Adams tank is approaching an almost deserted Horsted Keynes station from Sheffield Park. The land on the right is now occupied by carriage sheds, vital for keeping rolling stock out of the elements. Clearly car parking was not a problem then!

CHAPTER 11

THE ISLE OF WIGHT

In Autumn 1963, the Isle of Wight had lines from Ryde to Ventnor and via Smallbrook Junction to Newport and Cowes. Then the railway was run by a fleet of veteran ex LSWR 'O2' 0-4-4 tanks each bearing an Isle of Wight place name. The service was very good, bearing in mind the restrictions of single line running and would have made a superb working museum, had the locomotives and infrastructure been preserved intact. However, we are very fortunate today to be able to visit the preserved Isle of Wight Steam Railway where 'O2' 0-4-4T W24 *Calbourne* still runs. In 1963, a week's travel on the island's railways was made available by a weekly holiday ticket costing ten shillings (50p)! Such excellent value enabled numerous photographic opportunities, some of which are shown here. The end of steam on the island came on 31 December 1966, marking over a century of service by steam locomotives. Thankfully my visit in September 1963 came in time before the services became too run down.

Ryde St. Johns locomotive shed was built by the Southern Railway in 1930 and was alongside the northbound platform of Ryde St. Johns station. 'O2' 0-4-4T's 30 *Shorwell* and 33 *Bembridge* are at rest outside the shed. Note the enlarged coal bunkers for the island 'O2's; also the Westinghouse brake pumps and air reservoirs prominent on the left hand side of the locomotives. 1 September 1963.

'O2' 0-4-4T 18 *Ningwood* is approaching Ryde St. Johns station from Ryde Pier Head with a train of holidaymakers for Sandown, Shanklin and Ventnor. The line on the right provided a loop and access to a third platform face at Ryde St. Johns. 1 September 1963.

There was a useful footpath to Lake, an area south of Sandown station, where southbound trains could be observed on the stiff climb towards Shanklin. Here 'O2' 26 *Whitwell* is making the climb with a Ventnor train. 1 September 1963.

Ryde Pier Head station is host to two trains on 2 September 1963. Nearest the camera is 'O2' 36 *Carisbrooke* heading a Cowes train and on the other side of the water tank in Platform One is 'O2' 14 *Fishbourne* waiting to leave for Ventnor. First and last of the Isle of Wight 'O2' class together.

At Ventnor station, the tunnel under St Boniface Down provided part of the run round tracks for locomotives. Here 'O2' 0-4-4T 14 *Fishbourne* bursts out of the tunnel to pass the signal box to run towards its train to the right of the picture. In 1937, a train arriving at Ventnor was signalled into platform one, with a train already in occupation! Luckily the incoming train stopped in time. 2 September 1963.

It was a hefty climb to obtain this view! Steam is emerging from Ventnor tunnel as 'O2' 22 *Brading* is heading for its train, prior to departure for Ryde. This view is from St. Boniface Down overlooking the station and yard with the signal box adjacent to the tunnel mouth. 2 September 1963.

In the sunshine, 'O2' 32 *Bonchurch* is being serviced at Ventnor station which is 294 feet above sea level. Steam is still emerging from the tunnel. Coaching set 497 comprised a mixture of ex LBSCR and ex SECR vehicles. 6 September 1963.

The island platform at Havenstreet station, with a Ryde train departing in the distance pulled by 'O2' 35 *Freshwater*. The station building and loop were completed in 1926 to facilitate the expanding summer traffic. Havenstreet is the headquarters of today's Isle of Wight Steam Railway. 5 September 1963.

This is the terminus view at Cowes with 'O2' 35 *Freshwater* approaching the buffer stops with a train from Newport. 5 September 1963.

Cowes station was witness to an unusual shunting practice, which would undoubtedly be banned today! Once the locomotive had run round its train, the coaching stock was allowed to run to the bufferstops by gravity, with the locomotive following close behind before coupling to the train. In this picture, ex-LBSCR coach S4168 on the left, is moving into the station, with 35 following behind, about to pass the signal box. 5 September 1963.

A Ventnor bound train provides a useful viewing point to photograph Smallbrook Junction and signal box. The line to Ventnor is to the left and the line for Newport and Cowes to the right, whilst the signalman is about to provide the Brading tablet to the crew of 'O2' 31 *Chale*. The signal box usually opened in the summer season to allow double track running to Ryde for the expanded holiday traffic, whilst at other times, the box was switched out and the double track worked as two independent running lines. 4 September 1963.

Ryde Esplanade station is on a sharp curve where 'O2' 14 *Fishbourne* awaits departure for Ventnor. After departure, the train will travel sharply downhill to Ryde Esplanade tunnel. 4 September 1963.

On a sunny late afternoon, 'O2' 32 *Bonchurch* is entering Wroxall station with a Ventnor train. The fireman is ready to surrender the tablet for the section from Shanklin and to collect the tablet for Ventnor. 6 September 1963.

Now preserved 'O2' 24 *Calbourne* is at the head of a Ventnor train at Ryde Pier Head on Saturday 7 September 1963. Note the low departure signals for platforms 1 and 2 adjacent to the water tank. The ex-LBSCR bogie coach S4156 has recently been refurbished.

CHAPTER 12

THE LYMINGTON BRANCH

The Isle of Wight provided a stepping off point to reach another branch line. The ferry from Yarmouth enabled access to Lymington Pier station on 3 September 1963, whilst steam power was in charge of the Brockenhurst to Lymington Pier trains. The branch had opened in July 1858 to Lymington Town and to the pier in 1884. A new slipway was provided in 1938 and steam services ended in April 1967. Third rail electric trains ran the service from June 1967 and a modernised car ferry terminal opened in January 1976. It is good to note that this branch is still in operation today.

This is Lymington Pier railway station viewed from the Isle of Wight ferry TSMV *Lymington* which provided the ferry service from May 1938 until withdrawal in November 1973.

Ex-LSWR 'M7' 0-4-4T 30129, minus its shed plate, is at Lymington Pier station with a two coach push-pull train for Brockenhurst, with passengers from the ferry boarding. Connections at Brockenhurst could be made for London, Southampton, Bournemouth and to the Midlands via Broadstone and the Somerset and Dorset Joint Line to Bath. The 'M7's lasted until May 1964 on this service. The coaching stock is of Maunsell design. Note the unusual placing of 30129's smokebox door number plate.

As the train leaves Lymington Pier station, it provides a useful view of the station, the lower quadrant signals placed promptly to danger, level crossing gates and the ferry *Lymington* taking on board a Pickfords lorry.

The 'M7' 0-4-4T is backing the push-pull stock into Brockenhurst station prior to the next run to Lymington Pier. The 'M7' was allocated to Bournemouth shed in April 1963. 30129 was built at a cost of £1,605 at Eastleigh works and delivered in the second half of 1911.

The Brockenhurst train leaves Lymington Pier station with the 'M7' 30129 passing the Yarmouth ferry, *Lymington,* whilst people struggle to move a car that has refused to start. This 'M7' was withdrawn from service towards the end of 1963.

Lymington Junction signal box is depicted here from a train on the Ringwood line, the branch to Lymington Pier disappearing to the right. After electrification, the branch was re-routed behind the signal box and laid as a separate line into Brockenhurst to avoid interfering with main line traffic.

CHAPTER 13

BROCKENHURST TO BROADSTONE

This chapter provides the link between the Southern Region and the Somerset and Dorset Joint Railway (SDJR), which will be the location for the next chapter. After the 'M7' on the Lymington Branch had arrived at Brockenhurst, a review of the timetable showed a train for the Ringwood line, which then provided transport to Parkstone. A change of trains brought me back to Broadstone Junction, which provided an opportunity to see the junction to the SDJR in operation. These journeys were all taken on 3 September 1963. A large junction station had been built at Broadstone with four platforms in anticipation of traffic from the Midlands via the SDJR, Weymouth, Brockenhurst, Bournemouth and Salisbury. The SDJR's responsibility for track finished at Broadstone Junction and the S&D trains ran over LSWR tracks for the remaining eight miles to Bournemouth West. Broadstone station opened to LSWR trains in 1847 and SDJR trains first arrived here in 1872. The station was finally closed in March 1966 at the same time as the SDJR and there is no trace of the railway here as the area is now a housing estate.

This scene is at Brockenhurst before departing for Bournemouth via Ringwood. Rebuilt 'West Country' pacific 34040 *Crewkerne* is waiting to run round its train of two coaches and a van, prior to taking this huge load, tender first, to Parkstone via Ringwood and Broadstone.

BR '5MT' 4-6-0 73012, shedded at Bath, is entering Parkstone Station with a three coach Bournemouth to Bristol train via Broadstone and the SDJR. The first coach is an ex-LMSR brake. The line drops steeply from Parkstone towards Poole and climbs up to Broadstone which will be the last stop on Southern metals.

This view of Broadstone Junction shows the train headed by 'Standard 5MT' 73012 accessing the SDJR metals to head for Bristol. The line to Wimborne, Ringwood and Brockenhurst is to the right of the train. Lower quadrant signals on the Hamworthy line guard the junction, whilst the LSWR brick built signal box is unusual in its architecture.

Maunsell-designed 'U' 2-6-0 31802, one of the 'River' rebuilds, is passing Broadstone Junction with a freight service for the Wimborne line. Both routes depicted here lost their passenger services, the SDJR in March 1966 and the Wimborne line in May 1964.

CHAPTER 14

THE SOMERSET AND DORSET JOINT RAILWAY

Before embarking on the second part of this book, the Western Region, it is an appropriate moment to include some photographs from the well-loved line formerly known as the Somerset and Dorset Joint Railway as we move from the Southern Region to the Western Region. Both the Southern and the Western regions had influence over the SDJR so the line affords a very useful connection between the two parts of this book. Having just left school, I was able to visit this lovely line and it was fortunate that I took the chance before the rigours of working life restricted travel. All the photographs in this chapter are from 9 August 1963, the date of my visit. My journey commenced from Waterloo, on the 9.00am to Templecombe headed by rebuilt 'West Country' 4-6-2 34010 *Sidmouth* and the run was uneventful and punctual. The return was different. The 7.03pm from Templecombe to Salisbury was powered by 'S15' 4-6-0 30844 and from there the train to Waterloo was headed by rebuilt 'Battle of Britain' 4-6-2 34109 *Sir Trafford Leigh-Mallory.* We never reached Waterloo as there was a cable fire there and we all had to leave the train at Clapham Junction, having taken 90 minutes for the 5¾ miles from New Malden to Clapham Junction, causing a late return home! We now turn to the SDJR pictures.

The Western Region influence is evident as 'Pannier' 0-6-0T 3720 guides a Bournemouth bound train away from Templecombe Upper to rejoin the SDJR line for its southbound run. The 'Pannier' will be detached at Templecombe Junction allowing the train engine to proceed with its train. St Mary's Church is to the left of the picture and the school buildings complete the scene.

At the rear of the same train in the previous picture is 'Standard 5MT' 4-6-0 73047 backing towards Templecombe Junction to regain SDJR metals, where 73047 will become the train engine and take its coaches southwards. Note the rather fine Ford bread van in the foreground awaiting its next delivery.

Another Western Region engine, '2251' 0-6-0 3210 awaits a turn of duty on the Highbridge branch at Evercreech Junction as my train heads north towards Bath under the guidance of a splendid lower quadrant bracket signal.

A visit to the SDJR, however brief, was to enable a sighting of an ex-SDJR 2-8-0 in action. I had no knowledge of the timings for freight workings so it was a matter of being on guard during travel and station stops. I realise that this photograph would not be in the Ivo Peters' league of pictures, but it was an ambition achieved. Here, 53807 heads a southbound freight at the top of the climb from Shepton Mallet before it descends towards Evercreech (New). 53807 was the last ex-SDJR 2-8-0 in British Railways service, being withdrawn just over a year later on 5 September 1964. 53806 and 53809 were also observed on Bath shed later in the day.

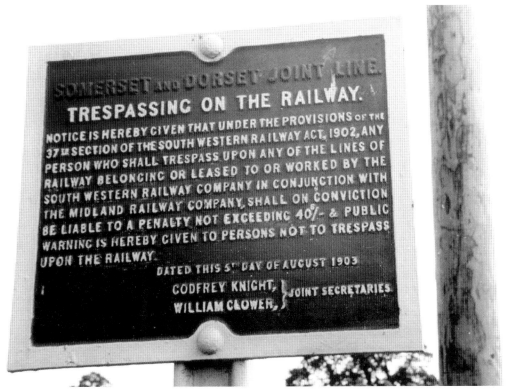

Another piece of SDJR history. A trespassers plate at Evercreech Junction.

BR 'Standard 4MT' 4-6-0 75007 enters Shepton Mallet station on a northbound local train. The locomotive's shed plate is rather crudely painted on, perhaps presaging its transfer to Yeovil in September 1964.

Shepton Mallet, Charlton Road station looking towards Evercreech Junction. 'Charlton Road' distinguished this station from the GWR High Street station. After their exertions over the banks, most southbound freight trains stopped here for water from the column by the starter signal at the end of the platform.

A notice by the SDJR specifying the use of fire bucket water, at Shepton Mallet station. Woe betide you for infringement!

Bournemouth shedded BR 'Standard 4MT' 2-6-0 76015 enters Shepton Mallet Station with the 5.08pm 'fast' train to Bournemouth. This train took me to Evercreech Junction, but I did not record any superlative velocity.

The final part of the journey on the SDJR was provided by double chimney BR 'Standard 4MT' 4-6-0 75071. Here it is entering Evercreech Junction with the three coach 5.53pm train for Templecombe. Note the first coach behind the tender is of Gresley design.

PART TWO
WESTERN REGION

CHAPTER 15

PADDINGTON

Where better to start the photographs of the Western Region than at its London Terminus? You might be forgiven for thinking that the Great Western Railway was still alive and well in that brass number plates, beading and safety valve covers together with copper capped chimneys, still abounded. Swindon locomotive works was continuing to refurbish locomotives to a very high standard represented by the sparkling exterior of locomotives 'ex works'. In the early 1960s there was still pride in the job, but change was not far away as modernisation took its toll of tradition. Paddington was home to the express classes of the Western, but also to hard working suburban tanks and pannier tanks, the latter in particular, heaving heavy empty stock trains to and from the carriage sidings.

I know perfectly well that this book is covering the British Railways period, but I could not resist the chance to include my father's photograph of 'Star' 4-6-0 4004 *Morning Star* about to back from Paddington arrival platforms towards Old Oak Common shed on 9 May 1931. Note the plethora of signs on the sides of the Goods Station. (*J.J. Knapman*)

Taken on the same day as 4004 is a picture of 'County' 4-4-2T 2223, awaiting its turn of duty outside Paddington station. The locomotives had 6ft 8½in driving wheels, the same size as a 'Star' or 'Castle' 4-6-0. The ride must have been somewhat enlivening! Note the end of a clerestory coach on the right. The approach signals to the terminus stare forbiddingly at the main line. (*J.J. Knapman*)

Back to the Western Region and double chimney 'Castle' 4-6-0 7003 *Elmley Castle* is striding purposefully towards the arrival platforms at Paddington with the up Cheltenham Spa Express, past the Goods Station, then displaying little or no signage. 15 August 1960.

Smartly turned out 'County' 4-6-0 1028 *County of Warwick* is arriving at Paddington with the 11.45am Bristol to Paddington train, including a first coach of LMS origin, as the empty stock of a train from Wolverhampton heads for the carriage sidings. 15 August 1960.

'Castle' 4-6-0 5044 *Earl of Dunraven* is in glorious ex works condition as it reverses from the arrival platforms at Paddington. Presumably it has been 'dressed' at the bufferstops for the 1.55pm Paddington to Neyland express with the headcode F46 and will be turned to take out that train later in the day. 15 August 1960.

In this picture, 'King' 4-6-0 6027 *King Richard I* is reversing out of Paddington's arrival platforms with the empty stock of the 7.30 am Shrewsbury to Paddington train, which it had brought to the terminus earlier. 15 August 1960.

I was under the impression that the 'County' class locomotives were not regular visitors to Paddington, but on 15 August 1960, a rather grubby 1024 *County of Pembroke* is piloting a nicely turned out 'Castle' 4-6-0 5032 *Usk Castle* with a westbound train. 5032 was at this time an Old Oak Common locomotive, which had its double chimney fitted in May 1959.

Somehow or other, the doyen of the 'King' class had arrived at Paddington as I had walked down Platform One to return home! This picture highlights the roof beams of the station and the bell carried by 6000 *King George V* is clear to see. The engine is quiet after its exertions with a train from Wolverhampton, with only a wisp of steam showing from the ejector. 6000 was an Old Oak Common allocatee and was withdrawn from service in January 1963 for preservation. 15 August 1960.

Suburban 2-6-2T '61XX', 6132 is seen here pulling a rake of empty coaches in to the departure platforms at Paddington. These 'Tanner Ones' as they were known, were popular performers on suburban services. 6132 is based at Southall and would last until October 1965. 7 August 1961.

Hawksworth 'Pannier' 0-6-0PT 9418, in filthy condition and carrying a duty 6 disc, comes in to Paddington's departure platforms with empty stock for a suburban service. 7 August 1961.

Majestic 'King' 4-6-0 6008 *King James II* is waiting to leave Paddington with a late afternoon service to the Midlands. The chalked headcode is unclear and probably relates to a working some days earlier. This Stafford Road locomotive would be withdrawn less than a year later. 7 August 1961.

Hawksworth-designed 'Modified Hall' 4-6-0 7919 *Runter Hall* is starting its train from Platform One in measured Western style. The chalked headcode on the smokebox refers to the 2.15pm Weston Super Mare to Paddington train and is obviously from an earlier working! 7 August 1961.

A further visit to Paddington on 1 April 1963 produced Worcester shedded 'Grange' 4-6-0 6806 *Blackwell Grange* on the 5.30pm train from Oxford. Whilst the picture quality leaves much to be desired, a 'Grange' must be something of a rarity at the Terminus during the decline of steam on the Western Region.

Nicely presented Old Oak Common double chimney 'Castle' 7032 *Denbigh Castle* is ready for departure from Paddington with the 6.35pm train to Cheltenham. Although the locomotive looks good enough for many years use, it was withdrawn in September 1964. 1 April 1963.

By early 1963, all the 'Kings' had been withdrawn and diesels were taking over the Western Region express services. However, it was possible to enjoy good runs to Reading, Oxford and Worcester behind steam, and double chimney 'Castle' 5056 *Earl of Powis* is about to back to Ranelagh Road depot to turn, prior to heading the 9.15am Paddington to Worcester train, which took me to Oxford, for a punctual arrival. 8 April 1963.

CHAPTER 16

OLD OAK COMMON SHED

On 30 November 1963, a pal and I decided to visit Old Oak Common shed. Why we chose that day, I do not recall as it was a depressing winter's day, foggy, damp and poor light. Given that so much Western Region steam was in the process of being withdrawn, our hopes would probably be dashed. However, two 'Castles' were present in steam to reward the visit and 'Clan' 4-6-2 72006 *Clan Mackenzie* was on shed after railtour duty, but locomotives inside the shed building were too dark to be photographed.

Worcester shed's 'Castle' 7025 *Sudeley Castle* is showing signs of life as it awaits its next duty. 7025 is in single chimney form and was withdrawn from Worcester shed in September 1964. It did unexpectedly participate in the Ian Allan high speed railtour of 9 May 1964 following the failure of *Pendennis Castle*. 7025 ran the Taunton to Plymouth section of the tour and acquitted itself well.

Coincidentally, the legendary participant of the 9 May 1964 tour, double chimney 'Castle' 7029 *Clun Castle* was the other 'Castle' 4-6-0 in steam at Old Oak that day. It stands proudly amidst the mist and neglect of the 1963 steam scene. 7029 was rescued for posterity and is now based at Tyseley where it has been refurbished for main line running. In the photograph, 7029 does not appear to have a shed plate, although it was then an Old Oak engine.

In the scrap line at Old Oak, rested withdrawn 'King' 4-6-0 6028 *King George VI,* which had been taken out of service a year earlier in November 1962. The dismal day reflects seeing a 'King' in this sorry state, having run 1.66 million miles.

Also in the scrap road was ex GWR mogul '63XX' 2-6-0 6379, which was one of the few '63XX' members without outside steam pipes. This locomotive had been withdrawn from Didcot shed after running for 1.33 million miles. A faithful railway servant.

CHAPTER 17

READING STATION AND SHED

On 1 April 1963, I had travelled via the Redhill to Reading line behind 'Manor' 4-6-0 7813 *Freshford Manor* to reach Reading South. (See Chapter Three). At Reading General, it was pleasing to observe named locomotives still in action, as I was only too aware from magazine reports that steam was heavily under threat at the time. 'Castle' 4-6-0 7014 *Caerhays Castle* took me back to Paddington on the 3.14pm departure, a Worcester train. A subsequent visit to Reading on 11 January 1964 was facilitated by 'Castle' 7005 *Sir Edward Elgar* on the 11.15am departure from Paddington. A kindly fellow enthusiast guided me to the shed for a pleasant visit to see engines of different classes still in steam. Inevitably, the weather was dull for both these visits, but I hope the contents of the photographs will be sufficiently enlivening.

Soon after my arrival at Reading Station, 'Castle' 4-6-0 7027 *Thornbury Castle* rushed westwards with a Worcester express. The headcode A22 indicates this train is the Cathedrals Express. 7027 was withdrawn in December 1963, subsequently arriving in Barry Scrapyard in June 1964. Tyseley Railway Museum rescued this locomotive, which has very recently been sold to a new owner, who has commenced restoration work on 7027. 1 April 1963.

A' Castle' sitting doing nothing? Reading Shed's 5038 *Morlais Castle* is attached to a van and is resting whilst on station pilot duty. Six months later, 5038 would be withdrawn from service. 1 April 1963.

'Manor' 4-6-0 7813 *Freshford Manor* was mentioned in this chapter's introduction and here 7813 is running light engine from the Southern line to go on shed at Reading (81D). 7813 would move to Swindon shed in 1964 followed by spells at Gloucester and Didcot before being withdrawn in April 1965. 1 April 1963.

A 'Manor' with a difference! Another of Reading shed's locomotives is also on station pilot duty having relieved *Morlais Castle*. 7816 *Frilsham Manor* is coupled to a tender bearing the GWR monogram, some fifteen years after nationalisation! 1 April 1963.

In the Southern Region part of this book, ex-Great Western engines had duties over Southern metals. Here we see the reverse position as Southern Region 'Q' 0-6-0 30541 travels tender first to its own territory. It had been allocated to Guildford shed in the previous month and presumably had been on a trip working. Note the large diameter chimney, which the locomotive no longer carries, 30541 having been preserved by the Bluebell Railway. 1 April 1963.

Before I adjourned to Reading Shed, 'Castle' 4-6-0 7005 *Sir Edward Elgar* departed for Worcester. Although the 'Castle' had performed well to Reading, it clearly needed attention with steam billowing from piston glands. 7005 would last in service for another nine months. The west end of Reading station is shown here with a crowd of enthusiasts in evidence below a lower quadrant bracket signal, whilst more modern motive power lurks in the background. 11 January 1964.

A delightful sight greeted the shed visitor as 'Castle' 4-6-0 5018 *St Mawes Castle*, shedded at Reading, was in steam awaiting its next task. It is in single chimney form, coupled to a Hawksworth tender and the whole ensemble is looking in reasonable condition. Sadly 5018 was withdrawn only two months later. 11 January 1964.

Two for the price of one! Suburban '61XX' 2-6-2T 6134 and 'Modified Hall' 4-6-0 7919 *Runter Hall* are both in steam at their home shed. 7919 is coupled to a Collett tender although a Hawksworth designed engine. 5018 and 7919 could have swapped tenders! Winter light is reflecting from the 'Hall' boiler indicating a degree of cleanliness. Reading Shed closed to steam in January 1965. 11 January 1964.

Severn Tunnel Junction allocated heavy freight locomotive '28XX' 2-8-0 2885 is the second in the Collett variant of this Churchward design. Various modifications, which included a side window cab, increased the weight of the original design by nearly a ton. The turntable is located behind 2885, with shed accommodation behind. 2885 is still with us, preserved at Tyseley Locomotive Works. 11 January 1964.

Oxley allocated '56XX' 0-6-2T 5606 is hidden away on a siding at Reading shed, having arrived on a freight working. These rugged 0-6-2T's were not often observed in the area local to London and presumably 5606 is in need of attention before returning home. Oxley shed became 2B from 84B in November 1963, when the shed became part of the London Midland Region. 11 January 1964.

'2251' 0-6-0 2257 is out of steam at 81D, parked in front of the water towers and coupled to a wooden ballast wagon. The locomotive still looks viable as it has a complete set of numberplates and it lasted until September 1964. 11 January 1964.

CHAPTER 18

OXFORD

Oxford GWR station was initially opened on 12 June 1844, after a branch had been completed to Oxford from Didcot. Although bypassed by the Birmingham services to and from London, Oxford nevertheless developed its cross-country network with services from London, Banbury, Worcester, Fairford, Swindon, Basingstoke and the South Coast, Princes Risborough, and Cambridge via Bletchley. Not only was there a variety of passenger services, but also extensive freight traffic could be witnessed. Oxford was a location where locomotives from all four regions could be seen. That variety was very nearly fulfilled on the occasion of my visit on 8 April 1963, which is the date of all the photographs in this chapter. Once more the weather was dull and misty; impossible to call out the sun! 81F Oxford shed closed to steam in January 1966.

To reach Oxford on 8 April 1963, the 9.15am Paddington to Worcester train provided the transport headed by double chimney 'Castle' 4-6-0 5056 *Earl of Powis* which competently gave an on time arrival. The carriage doors are still open as 5056 awaits departure from Oxford. 5056 was withdrawn in November 1964.

'Modified Hall' 4-6-0 6979 *Helperley Hall* heads a short freight working, southbound through Oxford Station. Two cement 'presflo' wagons are in the train, which is assumed to be heading for Hinksey yard. 6979 belonged to Banbury shed at this time.

Later on, '73XX' class mogul 7340 heads a lightweight load southwards. The locomotive is based at Didcot and it is probably returning to shed. 7340 was the penultimate GWR mogul to be built, a Collett variant of the class, with a side window cab. Note the plethora of signals in the distance and a locomotive moving in the shed yard.

Next on the scene was ex LMS '5MT' 4-6-0 45269 from Saltley Shed arriving at Oxford with the 10.15am Hereford to Paddington train. Its appearance on this service was due to a shortage of motive power at Worcester. It worked to Paddington and returned on the 3.15pm train, but it lost time on the return run. Note Oxford Station North signalbox and the 1959 erected signal gantry, where previously various bracket signals had sufficed. 45269's run was noted in *Trains Illustrated's Motive Power Miscellany*.

Oxford station was the location for engine change for the Pines Express from the South Coast. Here 'Merchant Navy' 4-6-2 35005 *Canadian Pacific* waits for the signal to leave its train, which would go forward behind a 'Castle' 4-6-0. 35005 has survived into preservation to run on the main line and is currently undergoing restoration.

Smartly turned out 'Castle' 7012 *Barry Castle* has taken over the Pines Express from 35005. A shame that the sun did not illuminate 7012's paintwork, but the Stafford Road allocated 'Castle' has plenty of steam and is ready to go. *Barry Castle* lasted until November 1964, but did not reach its namesake scrapyard.

This visitor to Oxford was the nearest I could manage to an ex-LNER locomotive as the class J94 0-6-0ST's closely resembled the locomotive pictured here. 'Hunslet' 0-6-0ST 3883 was the recipient of a new mechanical stoker and was undergoing trials to test the lessening of smoke emissions. Testing took place between Yarnton and Kingham with a load of thirty-eight four wheeled vans and the Hawksworth dynamometer car. The testing took place in April 1963 and here the locomotive is passing Oxford, bunker first. It was a day for unusual workings! Note in the background, a train in the Bletchley bay, a 'Black 5' headed parcels train.

Banbury shed's 'Hall' 4-6-0 6906 *Chicheley Hall* is arriving at Oxford with a local service from its home town. This picture shows more of the locomotive depot to the left, Oxford Station North signal box and the signal gantry. 6906 last served in April 1965. The real Chicheley Hall is located not far from Newport Pagnell and Bletchley.

'Hall' 6906 must have achieved a prompt turn round at Oxford shed to be ready to return to Banbury with a local service, as double chimney standard '4MT' 4-6-0 75008 passes on a northbound freight. 75008 was shedded at Oxford.

This southbound freight, with sheeted wagons at the head of the train, is led by '38XX' 2-8-0 3815 from 89B Croes Newydd shed. The bay platform's starter signal is prominent, with an interesting lamp at the top of the post carrying the Oxford station sign.

An up London express is slowing for the Oxford stop headed by double chimney 'Castle' 4-6-0 7013 *Bristol Castle*. The engine has an ugly lubricator attached to the smokebox side but retains the GWR conical buffer housings. 7013 was originally 4082 *Windsor Castle* but underwent an identity change with the then new 7013 to facilitate the use of 4082 on the funeral train of King George VI in 1952. In this picture, 7013 has lost its nameplate from the side in view, apparently stolen. 7013 was withdrawn in March 1965.

There was a good flow of freight trains through Oxford station on the day of my visit, as exemplified by double chimney '9F' 2-10-0 92228, northbound at the head of a rake of wooden bodied wagons. On this date, 92228 was allocated to Banbury. In the late 1950s, there were almost as many freight services as passenger trains passing through Oxford.

The dull weather emphasises the grubby appearance of Churchward-designed '28XX' 2-8-0 2836 as it heads north through Oxford with a tanker train. 2836 is allocated to Severn Tunnel Junction and was withdrawn in July 1964. Bracket signals for up and down trains can be seen at the south end of the station.

Rebuilt 'West Country' 4-6-2 34097 *Holsworthy* has arrived at the northbound platform with a train from Bournemouth to York. 34097 is about to go on shed and the fireman can be seen checking the signal is clear. It will return to its home shed of Eastleigh later with a southbound working.

Banbury shed's 'Modified Hall' 7905 *Fowey Hall* is bringing a York to Bournemouth train into Oxford under the north signal gantry, where a motive power change to a Southern Region locomotive will take place at the south end of the station, possibly to 34097.

Although Oxford Rewley Road station had closed, the yards leading to the station were still used for freight and Kettering shed's Stanier '8F' 2-8-0 48704 is shunting, whilst part of a 16XX 0-6-0PT is looking rather work shy! Earlier, Oxford shed's '16XX' 1630 had travelled light through the station to work in these yards.

Passing northbound is 'Hall' 4-6-0 6920 *Barningham Hall* with a fast fitted freight. Collett designed 6920 is coupled to a Hawksworth tender and the locomotive appears to have plenty of steam for its task. 6920 was allocated to 87B Duffryn Yard shed near Port Talbot, emphasising the traffic to and from Wales.

Time to go home! Old Oak's double chimney 'Castle' 7032 *Denbigh Castle* about to leave Oxford for Didcot and Paddington on the 5.30pm departure. My notes state that we had a very good run to Paddington, arriving five minutes early, a splendid way to round off the Oxford visit.

CHAPTER 19

TIVERTON AND HEMYOCK

On 24 February 1963, the Locomotive Club of Great Britain ran the Westcountryman Railtour. Ex-LNER pacific 'A4' 60022 Mallard provided the motive power from Waterloo to Exeter and from Tiverton Junction to Paddington. The journey between Exeter, Tiverton and Hemyock was provided with ex-GWR motive power, namely two '4575' 2-6-2T's and a 14XX 0-4-2T. It was a very cold day and a lively run ensued to Exeter with 60022, although the return was dogged with engineering work slowings. The '4575' 2-6-2T's hauled the special train from Exeter St. Davids via Stoke Canon and the Exe Valley to Tiverton, thence to Tiverton Junction, where those passengers lucky enough to hold tickets for the Hemyock branch changed trains to a train of two coaches and five brake vans, riding in which confirmed the intense cold, but it was well worthwhile.

The brace of '4575' 2-6-2T's, 4591 and 5564 are seen here in winter light at Tiverton. 4591 has lost its front numberplate, but otherwise looks tidy. 4591 was then shedded at Taunton, whilst 5564 had come from Swindon. Presumably Taunton could not spare two 2-6-2T's at the same time.

This time, 5564 is more prominent and the locomotives are looking towards Tiverton Junction, with the route signal already cleared. In the custom of the day, the enthusiasts have spread out across the tracks to take photographs. The route between Tiverton Junction and Tiverton was opened as a broad gauge line and converted to standard gauge in 1884. Both lines had closed by October 1964.

Taken from the train hauled by the two 2-6-2T's as they pulled into Tiverton Junction, is a view of 14XX 0-4-2T 1450, together with its train of two Eastern Region brake coaches of Thompson design, with five brake vans at the rear, prior to the journey to Hemyock. 1450 was shedded at 83C, Tiverton Junction, an Exeter sub shed, which closed in November 1963. We were just in time! 1450 has been preserved and is a pleasure to see in service on preserved railways.

Here, 0-4-2T 1450 has arrived at Hemyock Station. It has left room to run round its unusually longer train. The last passenger train on the branch ran on 7 September 1963. The Unigate milk factory at Hemyock provided milk tanker traffic for the branch until closure at the end of October 1975, the last milk train having run on the 28 October 1975.

CHAPTER 20

FESTINIOG RAILWAY SPECIAL 25 APRIL 1964

963 and 1964 were the years when the number of 'Castle' class locomotives was drastically reduced and so the chance to ride behind the well-known 4079 *Pendennis Castle,* famed for its locomotive exchange activities with the LNER in 1925, was too good to miss. The Festiniog Railway Special (FRS) had been an annual event for some years and the 1964 train not only provided 4079, but also the chance to ride the line from Ruabon through Llangollen to Morfa Mawddach, thence to Minffordd to connect with the Festiniog Railway. The Ruabon to Morfa Mawddach line closed early in 1965 after torrential rain undermined the track beyond economic repair. The known attractions of the tour were obvious, but little did we know that on the return, 'Castle' 7032 *Denbigh Castle* would fail at Birmingham, having crawled from Wolverhampton with a broken valve spring. Here, 7032 was replaced by a grubby 'Modified Hall' 6959 *Peatling Hall* which ran very well with the 452 ton train (including two sleeping cars) to arrive at Paddington on the following Sunday morning at 8.01 a.m. some 66 minutes late! 82 mph at Bicester and 69 mph at Seer Green were two of the highlights. A memorable journey!

On 25 April 1964, 'Castle' 4-6-0 4079 *Pendennis Castle* is backing on to the coaches forming the FRS at Paddington. 4079 was built in 1924 and withdrawn in May 1964, being subsequently preserved and now at GWS Didcot for extensive refurbishment. By the end of 1963, 4079 had covered 1.75 million miles. It was a Bristol, St Philip's Marsh resident.

Later, 4079 is seen at Shrewsbury station awaiting departure for Ruabon. The weather is dull (as usual!) but 4079 looks well and is waiting for the lower quadrant signals to clear. Much of the journey was in the seventies and 80 mph was recorded near Shifnal.

4079 is at Ruabon, where the train will reverse to join the Llangollen route. The 'Castle' has lost its special headboard and the express lamps have been changed. Pity authority trying to keep the running lines clear! 4079 had delivered the train to Ruabon at 12.21pm, on time.

The motive power for the journey to Minffordd from Ruabon was advertised as two 'Manor' 4-6-0's. In the event, two standard '4MT' 4-6-0's were provided being 75009 and 75023 both from Croes Newydd shed. 75009 lasted until the end of steam in August 1968. Here the pair is taking the train along the banks of the River Dee near Llangollen.

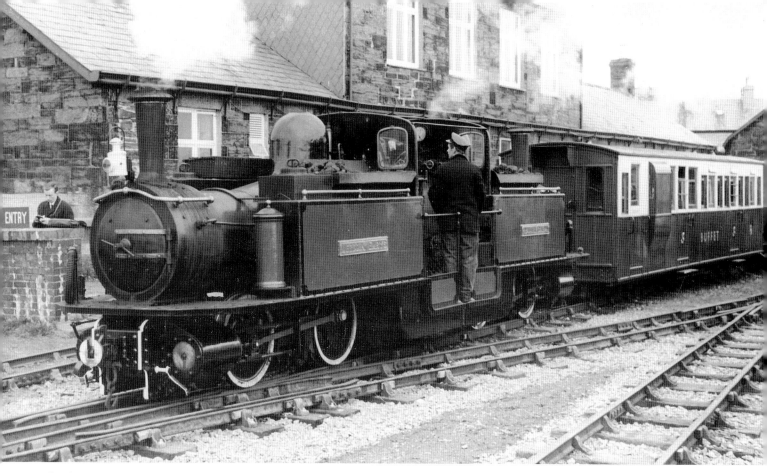

Just for the record, here is *Merddin Emrys*, the Festiniog Railway's 0-4-4-0T of 1879, at Portmadoc. Note the absence of cab roof. This locomotive is now the oldest working double Fairlie on the Festiniog Railway and is currently in service after an overhaul in 2016 and a return to coal firing from oil fuel.

26 April 1964. Just after 8am, Old Oak 'Modified Hall' 4-6-0 6959 *Peatling Hall* is backing out of Paddington with the empty stock of the *FRS*. 6959 did an excellent job as replacement engine and the driver reported that it ran well with plenty of steam available throughout. This had been a very long trip indeed!

CHAPTER 21

HEREFORD

In May 1964, the *Daily Telegraph* mentioned that the Oxford University Railway Society (OURS) would be running a special train being promoted as the Castle Class Farewell Tour, to run on Saturday, 16 May 1964. The tour would leave Paddington at 1pm and run via Reading, Oxford, Worcester, Colwall, Hereford, Pontypool Road, Severn Tunnel Junction, Pilning, Badminton and return to Paddington by 8.17pm! The locomotive throughout was 'Castle' 5054 *Earl of Ducie* which had run on the final leg of the Ian Allan tour a week before, when it had achieved 96mph. The OURS train comprised seven coaches including a twelve-wheeler cafeteria car, W9679W. The train ran early to most stops and the top speed at Honeybourne was 95mph (*Railway Magazine* log, July 1964), with stretches of continuous high-speed running. 325 miles in an afternoon! Reputedly it cost less than £50 to hire 5054 for the Tour. The chapter title is Hereford and as there was a 25-minute stop there, it enabled some useful photographs to be taken.

For the record, here is Worcester shedded 'Castle' 5054 *Earl of Ducie* backing on to the OURS coaches at Paddington. The reporting number Z48 had been used on the previous weekend for the Ian Allan special and 5054 is carrying the same number on 16 May 1964. The driver is carefully watching progress towards the coaches.

5054 is pictured at the south end of Hereford station's Platform Four. 5054 is still looking very presentable after its exertions of the previous weekend and it had produced some good running to Hereford with more to come. The sun is shining and glinting on the brasswork.

The Hereford stop showed that 'Grange' 4-6-0 6850 *Cleeve Grange* was sitting nearby, just waiting to have its picture taken. This Pontypool Road locomotive is hauling a class five vacuum fitted freight and 6850 is taking water prior to setting off after 5054 has departed. A four-wheel container wagon is at the head of the freight.

By complete contrast, a very grubby 'Castle' 5055 *Earl of Eldon* has arrived at platform three at Hereford. The locomotive is very grimy, the front number is chalked on and the shed plate refers to Cardiff Canton, but 5055 had been transferred to Hereford in March 1964. To finish the picture, the front coupling is hanging loose instead of being hooked up to the left buffer. 5055 is about to shunt the stock of this Worcester service for later use.

Two together! 41XX 2-6-2T 4107 is leaving Hereford with the 4.30pm train to Gloucester, whilst 6850 is blowing off impatiently, waiting to get its freight on the move southwards.

A ground level view of 5054 at Hereford. The neat OURS headboard has been placed on the top lamp bracket above the reporting number, Z48. The adjacent wagons are part of the train headed by 'Grange' 6850.

A final view of 5054 looking south, waiting for departure at 4.50p.m. The driver's white nameplate on the cab side reads Driver A. (Alf) Perfect, Old Oak Common. Driver Perfect was involved with the high-speed run of the previous weekend and certainly gave us some perfect running on this splendid afternoon run with 5054. A journey to savour! 5054 was withdrawn in October 1964. In the background is Ayleston Hill signalbox, governing movements at the south end of the station.

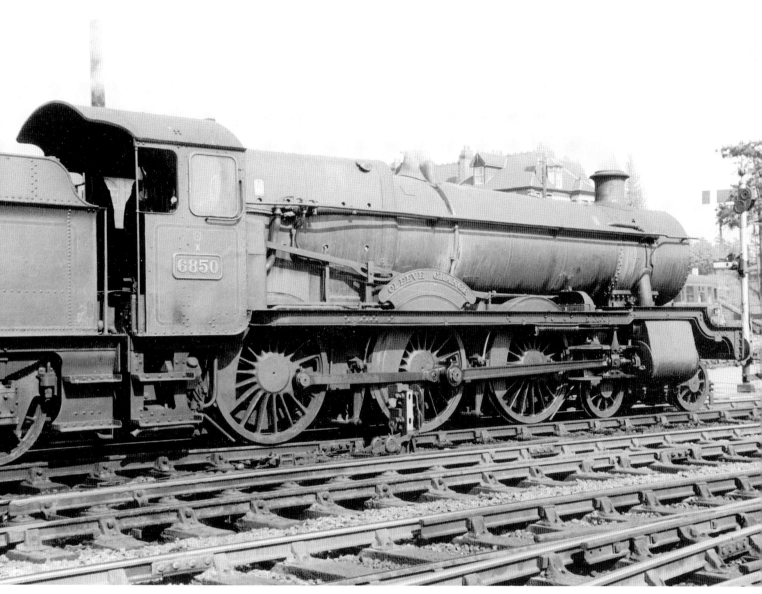

With 'Grange' 4-6-0 6850 *Cleeve Grange* at rest by 5054, it was a good time to take a close-up photograph of 6850. Although grubby, 6850 appears to be in good shape and will have to wait until 5054 has departed before the starter signal for the loop is lowered to allow the freight to set off.

CHAPTER 22

WELSH WEEK, JUNE 1964

With the inexorable decline of steam continuing apace, a pal and I decided to spend a week in Wales taking in as much steam activity as possible. This chapter will concentrate on the Western Region activities, although in November 1963, various Western Region sheds were transferred to the London Midland region, but those transfers will be disregarded for this chapter. Our travels encompassed Shrewsbury, Dovey Junction to Aberystwyth and as far north as Afon Wen. By June 1964, the majority of trains were powered by British Railways (BR) standard locomotives, but at least a 'Manor' held sway on the Cambrian Coast Express, although the headboard had been banished. I will let the photographs do the talking and they will be in date order.

The diesel hauled Cambrian Coast Express (CCE) gave way to steam at Shrewsbury and here is Machynlleth's (6F) 'Manor' 4-6-0 7819 *Hinton Manor* at the head of the *CCE* bound for Dovey Junction and Aberystwyth. 6 June 1964.

Having changed motive power at Dovey Junction, the Pwllheli portion of the CCE is approaching Barmouth Tunnel, headed by standard '3MT' 2-6-2T 82005. 6 June 1964.

On the 8 June 1964, standard '3MT' 2-6-2T 82000 enters Portmadoc station with a train for Pwllheli, which will take us to Afon Wen. These 2-6-2T's were popular with the crews.

On arrival at Afon Wen, the plan was to take the branch diesel to Caernarvon. Much to our delight, the diesel had failed, to be replaced by 'Black 5' 4-6-0 45223 with four LMS suburban coaches. Here 45223 is arriving at Afon Wen under a selection of Western lower quadrant signals. 8 June 1964.

45223 will work tender first to Caernarvon and here it is approaching its train at Afon Wen to couple up prior to departure, under a Western lower quadrant signal. Note the Ford Cortina parked nearby. 8 June 1964.

A rare glimpse of sunshine portrays standard '3MT' 2-6-2T 82003 passing the seaside at Afon Wen, avoiding the platform line, with empty stock for Pwllheli. 10 June 1964.

11 June would be a full Western Region day and so all the pictures to the end of page 137 are taken on that day. A dull morning greets standard '3MT' 2-6-2T 82000 arriving at Portmadoc station to take us to Dovey Junction.

En route, the train passed Talybont Halt, which was worthy of a photograph, due to its diminutive size.

The cloud is on the tops of the hills, but Barmouth Bridge stands out well, as our train approaches the bridge, which will carry us over the Mawddach Estuary.

Double Chimney '4MT' 4-6-0 75006, on a train from the Ruabon line, is held by signals at Morfa Mawddach as our train takes the coast line. Note the camping coach showing behind 75006's train.

BR standard '3MT' 2-6-2T 82000 en route for Dovey Junction, passes classmate 82020, northbound, at Morfa Mawddach. Three trains in one small station!

'3MT' 82000 makes the climb up to Friog avalanche shelter, passing a warning sign to down trains. Avalanche repairs can be seen beyond the tunnel and the telegraph pole route is prominent.

82000 has reached the coast line platform at Dovey Junction, having come across the trestle bridge to the right of the picture. Note the wooden plank platform extension.

Dovey Junction rush hour! On the left, standard '4MT' 2-6-4T 80131, a migrant from Tilbury and the LTS lines, with a train for Welshpool and London, whilst 82000 will take its now empty stock to Machynlleth, its local shed.

On arrival at Aberystwyth we were able to see the Vale of Rheidol railway's narrow gauge engine shed containing 2-6-2T 8 *Llewelyn*, at rest.

Whilst 2-6-2T 8 was at rest, sister engine 7 *Owain Glyndwr*, resplendent in green livery, was waiting to depart for Devil's Bridge. Note the use of a 6F shedplate. The Midland effect had arrived here too.

How not to present a 'Manor' 4-6-0? Gloucester, Horton Road's 7814 *Fringford Manor* is on shed at Aberystwyth, below the water tower and coaling point. This locomotive must have been 'borrowed' given its shed location.

7814 is about to depart Aberystwyth with the 5.40 p.m. service to Carmarthen. The 'Manor' seems to have plenty of steam and is attached to an intermediate size tender. Surprisingly, 7814 lasted until August 1965.

It is, of course, raining, but photography has to continue, as Machynlleth's 'Manor' 4-6-0 7807 *Compton Manor* is on station pilot duty at Aberystwyth. 7807 is much more presentable than 7814, although *Compton Manor* was withdrawn in November 1964.

Here is 7807 again, in Aberystwyth station platforms. The locomotive shed is behind 7807, whilst the Carmarthen line is seen curving away under a gathering of signals to the right of the picture.

The return to Portmadoc was interrupted by the customary train change at Dovey Junction, where '4MT' 2-6-4T 80136, (now preserved) having arrived from Aberystwyth, meets '3MT' 2-6-2T 82005, which has arrived from the Barmouth direction.

Our next steed would be '3MT' 82009, taking our train to Portmadoc. Here 82009 stops at Dovey Junction,
just beyond the then modern wooden signalbox. Travelling companion Richard studies 82009's valve gear.

Here is a closer view of the Friog avalanche shelter as '3MT' 2-6-2T 82009 climbs the hill in an easy manner. Its load of two coaches is not taxing.

82009 is about to enter Barmouth tunnel. The rock cutting above the tunnel begs the question whether a cutting was the first intention and then the tunnel has effectively been a fill in, which gives the trains some protection.

Ex-GWR motive power on the Barmouth line at last! This was the only non-BR standard locomotive in evidence on the line between Dovey Junction and Afon Wen. Machynlleth's '2251' 0-6-0 3208 is on empty stock duty at Barmouth station.

'3MT' 82009 is pictured at Barmouth station before setting off for Portmadoc, which was reached at 9.04pm! It had been a long day, but worthwhile to see some of the diminishing number of ex GWR locomotives.

For the return to London after the Welsh week of steam, '4MT' 2-6-4T 80104 brings the Pwllheli portion of the up *CCE* into Portmadoc station. 80104 is now preserved at the Swanage railway. 13 June 1964.

Now that is better! 'Manor' 4-6-0 7819 *Hinton Manor* has been spruced up to head the ten coach Cambrian Coast Express to Shrewsbury. My notes record a 'very enthusiastic crew' leading to a nine minutes early arrival at Shrewsbury. 13 June 1964. On 29 September 1991, we were able to relive the CCE experience when we rode behind 7819 from Aberystwyth to Shrewsbury with the Cambrian Limited special train.

CHAPTER 23

BARRY ISLAND

Steam had finished in August 1968 and it therefore seemed appropriate to visit the graveyard of steam locomotives at Barry Island on 14 September 1968. Was there any hope for these sad, dead engines at the time? Well, time was to prove a great healer and many of the locomotives departed Barry Island to a new life, a story which is well known.

'Hall' 4-6-0 4930 *Hagley Hall,* happily departed to the Severn Valley Railway.

'Castle' 4-6-0 5051 *Earl Bathurst* reached Didcot's Great Western Society centre and was a mainline performer for a number of years, now out of ticket at Didcot's museum.

'Manor' 4-6-0 7827 *Lydham Manor* does great work on the Paignton to Dartmouth railway.

A general view of some of the locomotives at Barry Island, many of which are ex Western Region.

CHAPTER 24

A GLIMPSE OF THE FUTURE!

The purpose of this book is not to record the preservation scene, but having struck a sad theme at Barry Island, it is good to finish on a positive note, by showing that steam was able to return to the main line.

Here are two pictures from 6 April 1974, when steam was in evidence on a special train at Shrewsbury station. Whilst the two engines concerned did not reach Barry, their return to steam was just as welcome.

'Castle' 4-6-0 4079 *Pendennis Castle* is about to move off to the Shrewsbury triangle to turn, with lower quadrant signals guarding its route.

The Rivals! With a few seconds to spare before departure, I was able to photograph ex LNER 'A3' 4-6-2 4472 *Flying Scotsman* and 'Castle' 4-6-0 4079 *Pendennis Castle* together at Shrewsbury. Steam is here to stay! Floreat Vapor!